Louisiana

AMERICAN

REGIONAL COOKING
LIBRARY
Culture, Tradition,
and History

African American
American Indian
Amish and Mennonite
California
Hawaiian
Louisiana
Mexican American
Mid–Atlantic
Midwest
Northwest
New England
Southern
Southern Appalachia
Texas
Thanksgiving

Louisiana

Mason Crest Publishers
Philadelphia

Mason Crest Publishers Inc.
370 Reed Road
Broomall, Pennsylvania 19008
(866) MCP-BOOK (toll free)
www.masoncrest.com

13 12 11 10 09 08 07 06   10 9 8 7 6 5 4 3 2

Library of Congress Cataloging-in-Publication Data

Louisiana / by Ellyn Sanna.
    p. cm. — (American regional cooking: culture, history, and traditions)
Includes index.
      ISBN 1-59084-615-X
      ISBN 1-59084-609-5 (series)
1. Cookery, American—Louisiana style. 2. Cookery, Cajun. I. Title. II. Series.
 TX715.2.L68H68 2005
 641.59763—dc22

              2004005291

Produced by Harding House Publishing Service, Inc., Vestal, New York.
www.hardinghousepages.com
Compiled by Ellyn Sanna
Recipes contributed by Patricia Therrien
Recipes tested and prepared by Bonni Phelps
Interior design by Dianne Hodack.
Cover design by Michelle Bouch.
Printed and bound in the Hashemite Kingdom of Jordan.

Contents

Introduction   6–7

Louisiana Culture, History, and Traditions   8

Before You Cook

     • safety tips   10–11

     • metric conversion table   12

     • pan sizes   13

     • useful tools   13–14

     • cooking glossary   14–15

     • special Louisiana flavors   16

Louisiana Recipes   17–67

Further Reading and For More Information   68

Picture Credits and Biographies   69

Index   70–71

Introduction
by the Culinary Institute of America

Cooking is a dynamic profession, one that presents some of the greatest challenges and offers some of the greatest rewards. Since 1946, the Culinary Institute of America has provided aspiring and seasoned food service professionals with the knowledge and skills needed to become leaders and innovators in this industry.

Here at the CIA, we teach our students the fundamental culinary techniques they need to build a sound foundation for their food service careers. There is always another level of perfection for them to achieve and another skill to master. Our rigorous curriculum provides them with a springboard to continued growth and success.

Food is far more than simply sustenance or the source of energy to fuel you and your family through life's daily regimen. It conjures memories throughout life, summoning up the smell, taste, and flavor of simpler times. Cooking is more than an art and a science; it provides family history. Food prepared with care epitomizes the love, devotion, and culinary delights that you offer to your friends and family.

A cuisine provides a way to express and establish customs—the way a food should taste and the flavors and aromas associated with that food. Cuisines are more than just a collection of ingredients, cooking utensils, and dishes from a geographic location; they are elements that are critical to establishing a culinary identity.

When you can accurately read a recipe, you can trace a variety of influences by observing which ingredients are selected and also by noting the technique that is used. If you research the historical origins of a recipe, you may find ingredients that traveled from East to West or from the New World to the Old. Traditional methods of cooking a dish may have changed with the times or to meet special challenges.

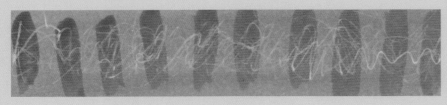

The history of cooking illustrates the significance of innovation and the trading or sharing of ingredients and tools between societies. Although the various cooking vessels over the years have changed, the basic cooking methods have remained the same. Through adaptation, a recipe created years ago in a remote corner of the world could today be recognized by many throughout the globe.

When observing the customs of different societies, it becomes apparent that food brings people together. It is the common thread that we share and that we value. Regardless of the occasion, food is present to celebrate and to comfort. Through food we can experience other cultures and lands, learning the significance of particular ingredients and cooking techniques.

As you begin your journey through the culinary arts, keep in mind the power that food and cuisine holds. When passed from generation to generation, family heritage and traditions remain strong. Become familiar with the dishes your family has enjoyed through the years and play a role in keeping them alive. Don't be afraid to embellish recipes along the way—creativity is what cooking is all about.

Louisiana Culture, History, and Traditions

Much of Louisiana's story begins long ago, far to the north. In 1632, three hundred French settlers arrived in what is today northeast Canada and Maine. There they worked together to carve out their homes in the wilderness. They called their new home Acadia.

But in 1710, Acadia became English territory rather than French. For the next forty-five years, the Acadians lived peacefully under British rule—but in 1755, they were expelled from their homes and forced to seek somewhere else to live. Despite the hardship and heartache they faced, they continued to work together as extended families. They refused to give up hope.

Some Acadians settled in nearby territories; some went home to France; others went to England. A large community, however, finally made its way to the French colony in New Orleans. There they at last found a new home. Today, about half a million people in Louisiana claim to be descendants of these brave and determined people. They have become an important part of a culture that is rich in history, music . . . and food!

Historic painting of Canadian scenery

Before you cook...

If you haven't done much cooking before, you may find recipe books a little confusing. Certain words and terms can seem unfamiliar. You may find the measurements difficult to understand. What appears to be an easy or familiar dish may contain ingredients you've never heard of before. You might not understand what utensil the recipe calls for you to use, or you might not be sure what the recipe is asking you to do.

Reading the pages in this section before you get started may help you understand the directions better so that your cooking goes more smoothly. You can also refer back to these pages whenever you run into questions.

Safety Tips

Cooking involves handling very hot and very sharp objects, so being careful is common sense. What's more, you want to be certain that anything you plan on putting in your mouth is safe to eat. If you follow these easy tips, you should find that cooking can be both fun and safe.

Example of a Louisiana-style home

Before you cook...

- Always wash your hands before and after handling food. This is particularly important after you handle raw meats, poultry, and eggs, as bacteria called salmonella can live on these uncooked foods. You can't see or smell salmonella, but these germs can make you or anyone who swallows them very sick.
- Make a habit of using potholders or oven mitts whenever you handle pots and pans from the oven or microwave.
- Always set pots, pans, and knives with their handles away from counter edges. This way you won't risk catching your sleeves on them—and any younger children in the house won't be in danger of grabbing something hot or sharp.
- Don't leave perishable food sitting out of the refrigerator for more than an hour or two.
- Wash all raw fruits and vegetables to remove dirt and chemicals.
- Use a cutting board when chopping vegetables or fruit, and always cut away from yourself.
- Don't overheat grease or oil—but if grease or oil does catch fire, don't try to extinguish the flames with water. Instead, throw baking soda or salt on the fire to put it out. Turn all stove burners off.
- If you burn yourself, immediately put the burn under cold water, as this will prevent the burn from becoming more painful.
- Never put metal dishes or utensils in the microwave. Use only microwave-proof dishes.
- Wash cutting boards and knives thoroughly after cutting meat, fish or poultry — especially when raw and before using the same tools to prepare other raw foods such as vegetables and cheese. This will prevent the spread of bacteria such as salmonella.
- Keep your hands away from any moving parts of appliances, such as mixers.
- Unplug any appliance, such as a mixer, blender, or food processor before assembling for use or disassembling after use.

Metric Conversion Table

Most cooks in the United States use measuring containers based on an eight-ounce cup, a teaspoon, and a tablespoon. Meanwhile, cooks in Canada and Europe are more apt to use metric measurements. The recipes in this book use cups, teaspoons, and tablespoons—but you can convert these measurements to metric by using the table below.

Temperature
To convert Fahrenheit degrees to Celsius, subtract 32 and multiply by .56.

212°F = 100°C
(this is the boiling point of water)
250°F = 122°C
275°F = 136°C
300°F = 150°C
325°F = 164°C
350°F = 178°C
375°F = 192°C
400°F = 206°C

Liquid Measurements
1 teaspoon = 5 milliliters
1 tablespoon = 15 milliliters
1 fluid ounce = 30 milliliters
1 cup = 240 milliliters
1 pint = 480 milliliters
1 quart = 0.95 liters
1 gallon = 3.75 liters

Measurements of Mass or Weight
1 ounce = 28 grams
8 ounces = 224 grams
1 pound (16 ounces) = 0.45 kilograms
2.2 pounds = 1 kilogram

Measurements of Length
¼ inch = 0.6 centimeters
½ inch = 1.25 centimeters
1 inch = 2.5 centimeters

Pan Sizes

Baking pans are usually made in standard sizes. The pans used in the United States are roughly equivalent to the following metric pans:

9-inch cake pan = 23-centimeter pan
11x7-inch baking pan = 28x18-centimeter baking pan
13x9-inch baking pan = 32.5x23-centimeter baking pan
9x5-inch loaf pan = 23x13-centimeter loaf pan
2-quart casserole = 2-liter casserole

Useful Tools, Utensils, Dishes

bread knife

cast iron skillet

griddle

egg beater

electric mixer

espresso maker

flour sifter

food processor

paring knife

potato masher

roasting pan

saucepan

colander

whisks

Cooking Glossary

clarified Made (as a liquid) clear or pure, usually by freeing of suspended matter.

cream To combine butter and sugar. This works best when the butter is room temperature, so take the butter out of the refrigerator at least an hour before you want to use it.

dash A few drops.

diced Cut into small cubes or pieces.

dredge Drag or toss meat lightly into a seasoning mixture; be sure to cover the entire piece of meat.

fold Gently combine a lighter substance with a heavier batter by spooning the lighter mixture through the heavier one without using strong beating strokes.

giblets The edible internal organs of fowl.

knead to work or press into a mass with or as if with the hands.

minced Cut into very small pieces.

pinch An amount that equals less than 1/4 teaspoon.

puree A paste or thick liquid suspension, usually made from cooked food ground finely.

roux A cooked mixture of flour and fat that's used to thicken soups or sauces.

sauté Fry in a skillet or frying pan with a little oil or butter.

simmer Cooking just below a boil so that the surface of the liquid just ripples gently.

stock A liquid in which meat, fish, or vegetables have been simmered, used as a base for gravy, soup, or sauce.

toss Turn food over quickly and lightly so that it is evenly covered with a liquid or powder.

zest A piece of the peel or thin outer skin of an orange or lemon used as flavoring.

Special Louisiana Flavors

bell pepper

cayenne

chilies

chives

garlic

green onions

okra

paprika

scallions

Louisiana Recipes

Chicken and Sausage Gumbo

Preheat oven to 350° Fahrenheit.

Ingredients:

¾ cup flour
1 teaspoon olive oil
18 ounces chicken breasts, halved
14 ounces smoked sausage
1 chopped onion
½ chopped green pepper
½ chopped celery stalk
2 cups hot water
¼ cup chicken **stock**
3 cloves minced garlic
10–ounce package okra

2 bay leaves
2 teaspoons dried thyme
1 tablespoon Worcestershire sauce
1 teaspoon hot sauce
½ cup chopped green onion
4 cups cooked rice

Cooking utensils you'll need:
small baking pan
large cooking pot
measuring spoons
measuring cups
paring knife

Directions:

Place flour in pan and bake in the oven for 15 minutes until the flour is the color of caramel. Stir every 5 minutes. Then brown chicken breasts and sausage in oil in a large cooking pot. Add and *sauté* onion, pepper, and celery. Sprinkle in browned flour, and stir in water and chicken stock slowly. Add garlic, okra, and seasonings. **Simmer** for an hour. Serve over cooked rice. (Remove bay leaves before serving.) Serves 8 people.

Tip:

Professional cooks keep chicken stock on hand to use in cooking, but in recipes like this you can use canned chicken broth instead.

Louisiana Food Traditions and History

The word gumbo comes from the African word for "okra." The slaves who came to Louisiana from Africa brought this vegetable with them. They used the okra to thicken soups and stews. Today, gumbo comes in many varieties, some with okra and some without. Traditional Louisiana gumbo is also thickened with filé (pronounced FEE-lay) powder, which is made from the dried leaves of the sassafras tree.

Although you can make gumbo with any sausage, the traditional Louisiana sausage is called "Andouille," a spicy, smoked pork sausage.

Cajun Blackened Chicken

Preheat oven to 350° Fahrenheit.

Ingredients:

cut-up chicken
Cajun Spice Mix (see page 24)

Cooking utensils you'll need:
large cast-iron skillet
large plastic bag
roasting pan

Directions:

Remove the skin and fat from the chicken pieces, and then rinse. Put spices and chicken pieces in a plastic bag and shake, so that the chicken is evenly covered. Heat oiled skillet over a high burner, and then put the chicken in the skillet. Cook for five minutes on each side or until the spice mixture turns dark. Remove the chicken from the skillet and place in a roasting pan. Continue cooking in the oven until the juices are clear when you pierce the chicken with a fork or knife.

Tips:

If you don't want to make your own Cajun spice mix, you can find it ready-made in most grocery stores' spice sections.

When using a skillet or frying pan, always remember to turn the handle so that it doesn't stick out where a younger brother or sister might grab it. When using a cast-iron skillet, the handle can become very hot, so be careful not to touch it with your bare skin.

Louisiana Food History

Chef Paul Prudhomme of K-Paul's Restaurant in New Orleans did a lot to make Cajun-style cooking popular in the United States. He was also the one who invented "blackened" food.

Prudhomme's signature dish at his restaurant was Blackened Redfish, which he made by dipping the fish in *clarified* butter, sprinkling it with Cajun or Creole seasonings, and then cooking it at very high temperatures in an iron skillet until a black crust formed on the fish. This dish became so popular that soon other restaurants were copying Prudhomme—and his technique spread to other meats as well. Some restaurants even offer "blackened hotdogs"!

Cajun Spice Mix

Ingredients:

5 teaspoons paprika
1 teaspoon dried oregano
1 teaspoon dried thyme
1 teaspoon cayenne powder
  (more if you like "hot" foods)
½ teaspoon black pepper
½ teaspoon white pepper
½ teaspoon garlic powder

Cooking utensils you'll need:
measuring spoons
small mixing bowl
an airtight container

Directions:

Mix spices very well and store in an airtight container.

Louisiana Food Traditions and History

Cajuns like their food well-seasoned—but not too hot. Black pepper and cayenne powder are found in most of their dishes.

Cayenne gets its name from the Greek word for "to bite." The cayenne plant was first brought to Europe from India in 1548, and it caught on quickly. Early Spanish settlers brought it with them to Louisiana.

Tips:

Cooking wine can be omitted from the recipe—but if you do use it, the alcohol cooks away as it is heated, leaving only the taste.

Never overcook shrimp or it will become tough and rubbery.

Serve Shrimp Sauce Piquant over hot rice.

Louisiana Food Tradition

Roux is the basis for many Louisiana dishes. It comes in three varieties—light (or "blond"), medium (or "peanut butter"), and dark. Creole cooks usually prefer a blond or medium roux, while Cajuns tend to like a very dark, smoky-tasting roux. Light roux only takes a few minutes to make, while a dark roux takes nearly half an hour.

Shrimp Sauce Piquant

*You may know this dish as Shrimp Creole—
but in Louisiana it goes by another name.*

Ingredients:

1 large finely chopped onion
½ green pepper
1 finely chopped celery stalk
*4 finely **minced** garlic cloves*
4 tablespoons vegetable oil
2 tablespoons flour
¾ cup cooking wine
*one 10-ounce can **diced** tomatoes
  with green chilies*
one 8-ounce can tomato sauce
one 14½-ounce can whole peeled tomatoes
1 cup water

1 teaspoon brown sugar
1 bay leaf
1 teaspoon dried basil
⅛ teaspoon paprika
1½ pounds shrimp, peeled
1 tablespoon Worcestershire sauce
¼ teaspoon cayenne
1 teaspoon pepper
***pinch** of ground cloves*
5 chopped scallions

Directions:

In a large cooking pot, *sauté* the onion, green pepper, celery, and garlic in 2 tablespoons of cooking oil over medium-high heat until soft (about 15 minutes). Mix flour and the remaining 2 tablespoons of oil in a small skillet to make a *roux;* cook over medium heat, stirring constantly, until the roux turns dark. Pour roux over sautéed vegetables and stir until vegetables are coated. Stir in wine, diced tomatoes, tomato sauce, whole tomatoes, water, brown sugar, bay leaf, basil, and paprika. Mix well and cover. *Simmer* for an hour, stirring occasionally.

    Toss shrimp with Worcestershire sauce, cayenne, and black pepper. Add to simmering sauce, along with the dash of cloves. Cook shrimp for a few minutes only. Add scallions and discard bay leaf at the last minute before serving.

Creole Vegetable and Braised Beef Stew

Ingredients:

3 tablespoons flour
1 tablespoon Cajun Spice Mix (see page 24)
2 pounds beef sirloin, cut into 1–inch cubes
3 tablespoons olive oil
1 **diced** large sweet onion
1 diced large red bell pepper
4 **minced** garlic cloves
1 cup dry red cooking wine
5 diced stalks of celery
4 thinly sliced medium carrots
one 10–ounce package frozen sliced okra, thawed
one 10–ounce package frozen baby lima beans, thawed
one 10–ounce package frozen corn, thawed

Cooking utensils you'll need:
large cooking pot
paring knife
measuring spoons
measuring cups

Directions:

Stir together flour and spice mix. **Dredge** beef in mixture. Then brown beef in hot olive oil in a cooking pot over medium-high heat for 5 minutes. Add onion, bell pepper, and garlic, and **sauté** for 2 minutes. Add wine, stirring to remove the browned particles from the bottom of the pot. Add the celery and carrot, and cook another 2 minutes. Then add the remaining vegetables and bring to a boil. Cover pot and reduce heat to medium-low. **Simmer** for 30 minutes. Makes 8 to 10 servings.

Tip:

Cooking wine can be replaced with water for this recipe—but if you do use wine, the alcohol cooks away as it is heated, leaving only the taste.

Louisiana Food History

Cajun? Or Creole? And what's the difference? The two words are like first cousins to one another—but their meanings are not exactly the same.

Creoles were the original descendants of the first French and Spanish settlers in this region. The word comes from the Spanish word criolla—"a child born in the colony." These people were once the "high society" folks of Louisiana. Modern-day Creole food is considered to be stylish and elegant. It includes French sauces and Spanish spices.

Meanwhile, the Cajuns started out as the original Acadian pioneers to Louisiana from Canada. Today, they are a mix of ethnic groups, including Spanish, French, Anglo-American, and American Indian. Cajun food tends to be simpler than Creole. It includes lots of seafood, and whole meals are often cooked together in one pot (like gumbo; see page 18). Some people say that Cajun food is "country food," while Creole is "city food."

Louisiana Food Tradition

Many Louisiana foods' flavors depend on the Louisiana "holy trinity"—onion, celery, and bell peppers.

Dirty Rice

Ingredients:

chicken **giblets**, wings, necks, and backs
1 quart water
1 stick of butter or margarine
2 cups uncooked white rice
2 cups chopped onions
2 tablespoons minced garlic
1 cup chopped celery
1 cup chopped green pepper
4 tablespoons chopped parsley
4 teaspoons Cajun Spice Mix (see page 24)

Cooking utensils you'll need:
paring knife
measuring spoons
measuring cups
2 large cooking pots

Directions:

Put the chicken parts in the water in a large cooking pot over a high heat. Bring to a boil and then lower heat and *simmer* for about 30 minutes. Skim off any scum that rises to the surface of the water. Let cool and then remove the meat from the chicken bones. Finely *mince* the meat and return to the water. Set pot aside.

Melt the butter over medium-high heat in another large cooking pot and add rice. Fry until the rice turns brown. Add onions, garlic, celery, green pepper, and parsley. Cook until the onions turn transparent.

Heat the chicken and broth again, and add to the rice. The water should be about one inch over the rice—you can add more water if you need to. Add the seasoning and bring to a boil over high heat. Cook until the water has almost totally evaporated and is just bubbling a little on top of the rice. Stir to prevent sticking, and then cover and cook over low heat for another 25 minutes. Remove from heat and let set for about 10 minutes. Stir rice well before serving.

Shrimp Remoulade

Ingredients:

1 cup ketchup
1 teaspoon hot sauce (more or less,
  depending on whether you like "hot" foods)
2 tablespoons mustard
2 teaspoons Worcestershire sauce
½ cup finely chopped green onions
¼ cup finely chopped parsley
½ tablespoon lemon juice
pinch salt and pepper
3 dozen boiled, peeled,
  and refrigerated shrimp
lettuce

Cooking utensils you'll need:
measuring cups
measuring spoons
mixing bowl
paring knife

Directions:

Combine all ingredients except the lettuce and the shrimp in a large mixing bowl. Cover and put in the refrigerator for at least four hours (preferably overnight—the longer the mixture sits, the more the flavors will mix together). Place a leaf of lettuce on each of six small plates, and put six shrimp on each lettuce leaf. Spoon a generous serving of sauce over the shrimp. Serves 6.

Louisiana Food Traditions

Shrimp Remoulade is a traditional dish during Carnival season in Louisiana. During this time, Louisianians eat, sing, dance, and have a good time. The celebration starts on Twelfth Night (January 6) and ends at midnight on Mardi Gras Day (the Tuesday before Ash Wednesday, which begins the Catholic season of Lent). The word Mardi Gras means "Fat Tuesday"—a time to enjoy as much food as you can before Lent's days of fasting.

Louisiana Food Traditions

According to Cajun folklore, when the eighteenth-century French Acadians made their way south from Maine and eastern Canada, they did not go alone on their long journey. When they lived in the north, lobster had become a staple in their diet—and the creatures were so loyal to the Acadians that they followed the travelers on their thirty-year trek.

Over the years, however, the lobsters became weary. Finally, they were so exhausted that they shrunk in size. By the time the travelers arrived in the swamps of Louisiana, the lobsters had turned into crawfish. The crawfish settled down with their friends the Acadians. The little sea creatures even built mud burrows that imitated the settlers' mud chimney.

And to this day, the crawfish will fight against all odds to survive. Like the Cajuns who still love to eat them, crawfish are famous for holding on stubbornly even in the most hopeless situations.

Crawfish Boulettes

Boulettes means "little balls" in French.

Ingredients:

1 pound crawfish tails (without their shells)
1 onion
4 garlic cloves
1 tablespoon dried or fresh parsley
6 green onions
1 cup bread crumbs
1–2 tablespoons of Cajun Spice Mix
  (see page 24)
4 beaten eggs (beat two in a small bowl,
  and the other two in another small bowl)
1 tablespoon Worcestershire sauce
hot sauce (use anywhere from a **dash** to a teaspoon,
  depending on how "hot" you like your food)
dash of salt and pepper
flour, cracker crumbs, or cornmeal for breading
cooking oil

Cooking utensils you'll need:
measuring spoons
measuring cups
food processor
mixing bowl
2 small bowls

Directions:

Put the crawfish tails, onion, garlic, parsley, and green onions in a food processor and chop fine. Pour mixture into a mixing bowl and add bread crumbs, Cajun Spice Mix, two of the beaten eggs, Worcestershire sauce, hot sauce, salt, and pepper. Mix together and shape into balls. Dip balls into remaining beaten egg and roll in breading (either flour, cracker crumbs, or cornmeal). Fry in hot oil until golden brown.

Jambalaya

Jambalaya (pronounced either jahm–buh–LIE–uh or jum–buh–LIE–uh) is a classic Louisiana one–pot meal that can be made a variety of ways—with chicken, sausage, shellfish, shrimp, ham, or even duck and alligator! This recipe is for a Creole–style "red" jambalaya (made with tomato sauce rather than meat stock only.)

Ingredients:

1 pound smoked sausage, cut into
   1-inch pieces,
   OR 1 pound diced smoked ham
1 teaspoon olive oil
1 large chopped onion
3 to 6 garlic cloves, minced
1 chopped bell pepper
4 celery stalks, chopped
3 small cans tomato paste
8 cups chicken stock
   (you can use canned chicken stock)

2 or 3 tablespoons of Cajun spice mix
   (see page 24)
2 bay leaves
1 28-ounce can tomatoes
salt to taste
1 pound cubed cooked chicken
   AND/OR any of the following in
   combination:
   1 pound peeled shrimp
   1 pound of any kind of poultry
   1 pound fish, cubed
   1 pound of shellfish
4 cups uncooked white rice

Directions:

In a frying pan or skillet, brown the sausage and pour off extra fat. In the same pan, sauté the onions, garlic, peppers, and celery in oil until onions begin to turn transparent. Then add the tomato paste and let it brown a little. Stir constantly so it doesn't burn. Add about 2 cups of the stock to the mixture, scraping the bottom of the pan to mix up any browned bits, and stir until smooth, making sure the sautéed vegetables, paste and stock are combined thoroughly. Add the spices, tomatoes, and salt. Cook over low-medium heat for about 10

minutes. Then add the meat and/or seafood and cook another 10 minutes. (If you're using seafood, be careful not to overcook it.) Add the rest of the stock and stir in the rice. Cook for about 20-25 minutes, or until the rice has absorbed all the liquid and is cooked through. Stir thoroughly to combine all ingredients. Remove bay leaves before serving.

Tip:

If you serve jambalaya with a salad and a loaf of French bread, you have an easy complete meal.

Louisiana Food Tradition

Monday is the traditional day to eat this dish. In the old days in Louisiana, women did their laundry on Mondays. Before automatic washers and dryers, washing clothes was an all-day job. Women would start the beans in the morning, and let them cook all day. By the time the laundry was done, so was supper. Many restaurants in New Orleans still serve Red Beans and Rice on Mondays.

Red Beans and Rice

Ingredients:

1 pound dry red beans
1 meaty hambone
  (trim off any fat)
2 large chopped onions
1 chopped green pepper
2 chopped celery stalks
2 finely chopped
  cloves of garlic

pinch of salt and pepper
pinch of sugar
1 bay leaf
2 pounds spicy sausage links
¼ cup chopped parsley
3 cups cooked rice

Directions:

Soak beans in pot of water overnight. Pour off water and add hambone to the beans, along with onion, green pepper, celery, garlic, salt, pepper, sugar, and bay leaf. Cover with water and cook over medium heat. Meanwhile, boil the sausage in a skillet, in enough water to cover it, for 10 minutes. Drain off water and fry until crisp, then set aside. After 1 to 2 hours, when beans feel soft when they're poked with a fork, add the sausage to the bean pot. Just before serving, remove the bay leaf, and add parsley. Serve over rice.

Tips:

If you don't have time to soak your beans overnight, bring them to a full boil in just enough water to cover them. Boil for five minutes, to soften shells, and then proceed with the rest of the recipe.

People in Louisiana often serve this dish with corn bread and mustard greens.

New Orleans Muffaletta

Ingredients:

⅓ cup finely chopped red bell pepper
¼ cup finely chopped black olives
3 tablespoons chopped parsley
½ teaspoon dried basil
½ teaspoon dried oregano
1 baguette (loaf of French bread
  about 14 inches long)
4–6 lettuce leaves
4–6 ounces thinly sliced roast beef
4–6 ounces thinly sliced provolone cheese
4–6 ounces sliced Genoa salami
4–6 ounces Swiss cheese
4–6 ounces sliced mortadella
12 sliced-for-sandwiches dill pickle slices

Cooking utensils you'll need:
measuring cups
measuring spoons
small mixing bowl
bread knife

Directions:

Combine the first five ingredients in a small bowl and mix. Cut baguette in half and then cut each half horizontally. Spread mixture on each slice of bread. Layer on lettuce, meat, and cheese. Top with pickle slices, and gently press top piece of bread on top. Sandwiches' flavor improves if they sit for a half hour or so before eating.

Tips:

This recipe calls for fresh parsley, but you can substitute 1⅓ tablespoons dried parsley.

If you don't like mortadella—or you can't find it—you can use bologna instead.

Louisiana Tradition

During the Carnival season, "krewes"—private social organizations—sponsor the many parades that troop through the streets. People in masks and costumes throw colorful beads, "gold" doubloons, and other goodies from the parade floats, while the crowd chants, "Throw me something!" Night parades are often lit by dancers carrying torches.

When it is still dark on Mardi Gras morning, people in costumes set out picnic tables and barbecue pits along parade routes. They spread out blankets and baskets filled with food and drink, and they set up stepladders so that they will be in the best possible position to catch "throws." People spend the day visiting with friends and watching parades and the other costumed revelers.

Louisiana Food Tradition

One of the most famous holidays in the world is the New Orleans Mardi Gras. Each year more than $950 million is spent on the event—and more than half a million people from all around the world come to join the celebration.

Green Salad with Creole Vinaigrette

Ingredients:

1 medium, finely **minced** shallot
2 ounces vinegar
3 ounces olive oil
3 ounces walnut oil
3 or 4 drops of hot sauce
  (more or less depending on your taste)
1 tablespoon spicy mustard
pinch of salt and pepper
mixed greens
2 or 3 tomatoes, cut in quarters
1 thinly sliced red onion

Cooking utensils you'll need:
paring knife
whisk
mixing bowl
liquid measuring cups
(these will be marked
with ounces as well as cups)
measuring spoons

Directions:

Combine the shallots, vinegar, olive oil, walnut oil, hot sauce, and mustard. Whisk slowly until thoroughly mixed; add salt and pepper. Serve over greens and tomatoes, with red onions in the center.

Quiche Lorraine

Quiche is good for breakfast, brunch, lunch, or a light supper.

Preheat oven to 425° Fahrenheit.

Cooking utensils you'll need:
measuring cups
measuring spoons
mixing bowl

Ingredients:

9-inch pastry piecrust
8 slices of bacon,
  cooked until crisp and crumbled
1 cup shredded Swiss cheese
1 cup minced onion

4 large eggs
2 cups heavy cream
¼ teaspoon salt
¼ teaspoon pepper
⅛ teaspoon cayenne pepper

Directions:

Sprinkle the bacon, cheese, and onion in the bottom of the piecrust. Beat eggs slightly with the remaining ingredients and pour mixture into the pie shell. Bake 15 minutes and then reduce oven temperature to 300 degrees Fahrenheit, and cook another 30 minutes—or until a knife inserted into the center of the quiche comes out clean. Let stand for 10 minutes before cutting.

Tips:

You can buy ready-made piecrusts at the grocery store.

If you like, you can cook bacon in the microwave instead of a frying pan. Put the bacon slices on several paper towels to absorb the fat.

1 cup shredded cheese = 4 ounces

For a less rich, low-fat alternative, use skim milk instead of heavy cream.

Louisiana Food History

Although quiche is now a classic French dish, quiche actually comes from Germany—the medieval kingdom of Lothringen, which the French later renamed Lorraine. The word *quiche* comes from the German word kuchen, meaning cake. The original quiche was an open pie with a custard and bacon filling. Later, cheese was added, and then onions. The bottom crust was originally made from bread dough, but that eventually evolved into a piecrust.

Quiche became popular in the United States during the 1950s. Because it lacked hearty meat ingredients, people often thought of it as a feminine dish—which led to the saying, "Real men don't eat quiche." Today, however, quiche is popular in Louisiana with almost everyone. It comes in many varieties, including broccoli, mushroom, and seafood. Quiche can be served as an appetizer or as a main dish for breakfast, lunch, or a light supper.

Louisiana Food History

Although Pain Perdu is a French version of French toast, French toast really isn't French at all. In fact, it might better be called "American toast" or even "New York State toast."

The first French toast was made in 1724 at a roadside tavern not far from the city of Albany. The name of the tavern's owner was Joseph French, and he gave his name to his food invention. Pain Perdu is a more recent dish, adapted from this early American breakfast treat.

Pain Perdu

*Another good breakfast food, this is "French toast,"
the way New Orleans' French descendants eat it.
The French words mean "Lost Bread." It's a good
way to use up stale bread.*

Cooking utensils you'll need:
large mixing bowl
measuring cups
measuring spoons
large skillet, frying pan, or griddle

Ingredients:

4 large well-beaten eggs
1 cup milk
¼ cup sugar
2 teaspoons vanilla
pinch of nutmeg
8 slices stale French bread
* (cut about 1-inch thick)*

4 tablespoons butter
4 tablespoons vegetable oil
2 teaspoons powdered sugar,
* mixed with ½ teaspoon cinnamon*

Directions:

Mix the eggs with the milk, sugar, vanilla, and nutmeg. Then soak the slices of French bread in the egg mixture until the bread is thoroughly soaked. Meanwhile, melt the butter in the skillet, frying pan, or griddle, and add the oil. When the mixture is very hot, fry the bread slices one or two at a time, until each side is golden brown. (You will need to flip them over with a pancake turner.) Drain on paper towels and keep in a warm oven (200° Fahrenheit) until all the slices are cooked. Sprinkle with the powdered sugar and cinnamon mixture just before serving. Serves 4 people (2 slices each).

Tips:

If you don't have French bread, use sliced Italian bread or any other firm-textured white bread.

Pain Perdu is good with maple syrup or honey. In Louisiana, it's often served with cane syrup, a sweet syrup made from cooking sugar cane.

Strawberry Sorbet

Sorbet is a little like homemade sherbet. It's often served as a dessert—or between spicy main dishes to "clean the palate."

Ingredients:

1 cup sugar
2 cups water
2 quarts fresh strawberries
2 tablespoons lemon juice

Cooking utensil you'll need:
measuring cups
measuring spoons
saucepan
food processor
strainer
ice cream freezer

Directions:

Stir sugar and water together in a saucepan and *simmer* about 10 minutes until a syrup forms. Add the strawberries and lemon juice, and *puree* the mixture in a food processor. Remove the seeds and pulp by straining the mixture through a fine strainer. Press down hard on the solids in the strainer to extract all the juice. Place the strained juice in an ice cream freezer, according to the freezer directions, and freeze until firm. Makes about 12 scoops.

Chocolate Doberge Cake

Preheat oven to 300° degrees Fahrenheit.

Ingredients:

Batter
2 cups sifted flour
1 teaspoon baking soda
1 teaspoon salt
10 tablespoons butter
1 ½ cups sugar
3 eggs, separated, with the
   whites beaten until stiff
1 cup buttermilk
1 ½ squares of melted
   unsweetened baking chocolate
1 ¼ teaspoons vanilla
1 teaspoon almond extract

Filling
2 ½ cups evaporated milk
two 1-ounce squares
   of dark chocolate candy bar
1 ¼ cups sugar
5 tablespoons flour
4 egg yolks
2 tablespoons butter
1 ¼ teaspoons vanilla
¼ teaspoon almond extract

Frosting
1 ¼ pounds of sugar (about 3 cups)
1 cup evaporated milk
2 ounces (two squares) baking
   chocolate
4 tablespoons butter
1 teaspoon vanilla

Cooking utensils you'll need:
measuring cups
measuring spoons
mixing bowls
egg beater or electric mixer
flour sifter
two 9-inch round cake pans
saucepans

Chocolate Doberge Cake (continued)

Directions:

Sift the flour, baking soda, and salt together in a medium-sized mixing bowl. In a large mixing bowl, *cream* the butter and sugar together, and add the egg yolks one at a time. Gradually, add the flour mixture and the buttermilk, alternating between the two. Then add the chocolate and beat with a mixing spoon for about 3 minutes. *Fold* in the beaten egg whites, the vanilla, and the almond extract. Grease and flour two 9-inch round cake pans, and pour batter into pans. Bake for 45 minutes. After the cake cools, carefully split each layer into two to make four layers.

To make the filling, heat the milk and chocolate over medium-high heat until the chocolate is melted. Combine sugar and flour in a medium-sized mixing bowl. Make a paste by adding the hot chocolate a little at a time to the sugar and flour. Then return the entire chocolate mixture to the saucepan and stir over medium heat until thick. Add the 4 egg yolks and stir rapidly until completely blended. Cook for another 2 or 3 minutes, and then remove from the heat. Add butter, vanilla, and almond extract, and let the mixture cool in the refrigerator. When both the cake and the filling are cool, use a table knife or spatula to spread the filling on the first layer of the cake. Place the second layer on top of the first layer, and cover its top with filling, and then the third layer. Do not spread filling on the topmost layer.

For the frosting, combine milk and sugar in a saucepan and bring to a boil over high heat, stirring constantly. Reduce heat and *simmer* for 6 minutes without stirring. Remove from the stove and blend in chocolate. Add butter and vanilla, and return to medium-low heat to cook for another 1 or 2 minutes stirring constantly. Remove from stove and place in the refrigerator to cool. When completely cool, beat the frosting with a mixing spoon and then spread on the top and sides of the cake.

Tips:

You can substitute margarine for butter in most recipes.

Semisweet chocolate chips can be used instead of a dark chocolate candy bar.

If you don't have buttermilk, you can add a teaspoon and a half of vinegar to a cup of regular milk to achieve the same chemical reaction that the buttermilk has with the baking soda. But don't try to make this recipe with plain regular milk and don't try to substitute baking powder for baking soda. Baking powder and baking soda are both "leavening agents"—that means they make batter rise when it's cooked—but baking soda requires an acid in order to work (such as that found in buttermilk, sour milk—or vinegar), while baking powder has the acid already included.

A good way to tell if a cake is ready to come out of the oven is to poke the center with a toothpick. If the toothpick comes out clean, the cake is done.

Don't ever try to frost a cake until both the cake and the icing is completely cooled. Otherwise, you'll end up with a slippy-sloppy mess of frosting and crumbs!

Louisiana Food History

This typical New Orleans cake gets its name from a French word that means "Innkeeper's Cake." Traditionally, the cake is very tall, with eight layers, but this is "beginner's" Doberge Cake, with only four layers. If you want to try it with eight layers, you'll have to double the recipe. It's a very rich, very fancy cake that takes lots of work to make—but this special Louisiana dessert is well worth the effort.

Chocolate Bourbon Pecan Pie

Preheat oven to 325° Fahrenheit.

Ingredients:

Cooking utensils you'll need:
measuring cups
measuring spoons
mixing bowl
small saucepan

1 ready-made 9-inch piecrust
1 cup white sugar
1 cup light corn syrup
½ cup butter
4 beaten eggs
¼ cup bourbon
1 teaspoon vanilla

¼ teaspoon salt
6 ounces semisweet chocolate chips
1 cup chopped pecans

Directions:

In a small saucepan combine sugar, corn syrup, and butter (or margarine), and cook over medium heat, stirring constantly, until butter melts and sugar dissolves. Cool slightly. Combine eggs, bourbon, vanilla, and salt in a large mixing bowl. Slowly pour the sugar mixture into the egg mixture and blend. Stir in chocolate chips and pecans, and then pour mixture into the piecrust. Bake 50 to 55 minutes, until the filling is firm (it shouldn't "jiggle" if you touch it with a spoon) and the crust golden.

Tips:

You can make almost any pie recipe in small, tart-sized crusts instead of large pies—but if you do, be sure to decrease the amount of time you leave it in the oven, as small tarts cook faster than large pies.

Most of the alcohol in the bourbon will cook away, leaving only the flavor, but you can also replace it with ¼ cup water and 1 teaspoon rum-flavored extract.

Louisiana Food History

Many people connect the word "bourbon" with New Orleans and Louisiana. That's because Bourbon Street is one of the most famous addresses in the world. Surprisingly, though, the street was not originally named after the whiskey by the same name. Instead, the street was named in the early days of New Orleans after the French Royal Family, the House of Bourbon.

In those days, Bourbon Street was a prestigious residential street—but today it's famous for its jazz clubs, bars, and souvenir shops. During the day, Bourbon Street is not much different from any street in New Orleans' French Quarter. As night falls, however, and the lights come on, the street comes alive with crowds of partygoers. Music spills from the bars and clubs, and voices shout out from the doorways, persuading passersby to enter.

King Cake

This traditional Mardi Gras dessert is really more of a sweet bread than a cake.

Preheat oven to 375° degrees Fahrenheit.

Ingredients:

Bread
½ cup warm water
2 tablespoons yeast
½ cup plus 2 teaspoons sugar
3 ½ to 4 cups flour
1 teaspoon nutmeg
2 teaspoons salt
1 teaspoon lemon zest
½ cup warm milk
5 egg yolks

½ cup butter, softened
2 teaspoons cinnamon
small plastic baby
  (available at hobby stores)

Icing:
3 cups confectioner's sugar
¼ cup lemon juice
3 to 6 tablespoons water
colored sprinkles

Directions:

Sprinkle the yeast and 2 teaspoons of sugar over warm water in a small bowl. Allow it to sit for 3 to 5 minutes and then mix thoroughly. Set the bowl in a warm place for about 10 minutes until the yeast bubbles.

In a large mixing bowl, mix together 3 ½ cups flour, the remaining sugar, nutmeg, lemon zest, and salt. Gradually, add yeast mixture, milk, egg yolks, and softened butter. Add more flour as need to make a soft ball. *Knead* the dough for about 10 minutes until it is shiny and stretchy. Place dough in a buttered bowl and cover, then set in a warm place for about 1 ½ hours until the dough doubles in size.

When dough has risen, punch down and sprinkle with the cinnamon. Form the dough into a cylinder shape and twist it into a circle. Pinch the ends together to complete the circle. Cover again and allow to rise for about 45 more minutes, until doubled in size. Bake for 25–35 minutes, until it is golden brown.

When the cake is completely cool, poke the plastic baby into it. The hole will be hidden once you frost the top of the cake with the icing. Mix together the confectioner's sugar, lemon juice, and enough water to make smooth, spreadable icing. Decorate with sprinkles.

Louisiana Food History

King Cake is an ancient tradition that stretches back to medieval celebrations of Twelfth Night or Epiphany, twelve days after Christmas when something wonderful—the Christ Child—was revealed to the three kings who followed the star from the East. In the Middle Ages across England and France, people hid a surprise in a cake, a tiny treasure for one lucky guest, as a way of reenacting the events of Epiphany. The French developed the custom of hiding a bean-sized Baby Jesus in the pastry. The cakes became round and were decorated to look like a crown, in memory of the King of Heaven. Eventually, a new tradition was added: whoever found the baby in his or her piece of cake, was king- or queen-for-the-day.

In Louisiana today, King Cakes play an important role in the Carnival season. They are often elaborately decorated with green, purple, and gold, the colors of Mardi Gras. According to tradition, whoever gets the baby has to throw a Carnival party the next year.

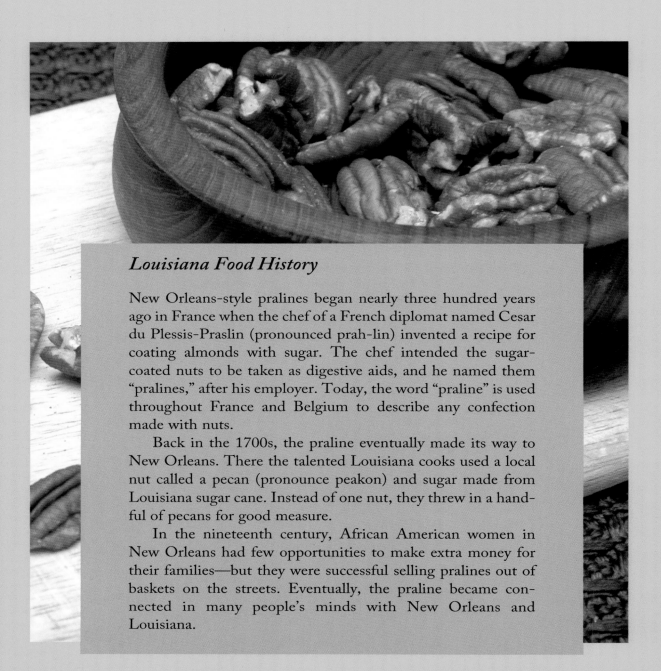

Louisiana Food History

New Orleans-style pralines began nearly three hundred years ago in France when the chef of a French diplomat named Cesar du Plessis-Praslin (pronounced prah-lin) invented a recipe for coating almonds with sugar. The chef intended the sugar-coated nuts to be taken as digestive aids, and he named them "pralines," after his employer. Today, the word "praline" is used throughout France and Belgium to describe any confection made with nuts.

Back in the 1700s, the praline eventually made its way to New Orleans. There the talented Louisiana cooks used a local nut called a pecan (pronounce peakon) and sugar made from Louisiana sugar cane. Instead of one nut, they threw in a handful of pecans for good measure.

In the nineteenth century, African American women in New Orleans had few opportunities to make extra money for their families—but they were successful selling pralines out of baskets on the streets. Eventually, the praline became connected in many people's minds with New Orleans and Louisiana.

Pecan Pralines

Ingredients:

¾ cup brown sugar
¾ cup white sugar
½ cup evaporated milk
½ teaspoon vanilla
2 tablespoons butter
1 cup pecans

Cooking utensils you'll need:
measuring cups
measuring spoons
heavy saucepan
wooden spoon
waxed paper

Directions:

Combine sugar and milk, and cook in heavy saucepan over low heat until the mixture thickens into a soft ball. Remove from stove and add the butter, vanilla, and pecans. Beat mixture with a wooden spoon until it looks smooth and creamy. Then drop by spoonfuls onto waxed paper. If the candy does not harden within 10 minutes, you may need to cook it some more. Makes about 1 dozen pralines.

Café au Lait

Ingredients:

1 cup of espresso coffee
4 cups of milk
sugar
cinnamon

Directions:

Cooking utensils you'll need:
measuring cups
coffeemaker
saucepan

Make the espresso, either using a special
espresso maker or a regular coffeemaker. (Be
sure to follow the directions on the can as to amounts of coffee and water.)
Heat the milk, either in a saucepan on the stove or in individual mugs, one
at a time in the microwave. Add about ¼ cup espresso to each mug of milk.
Stir and add sugar as desired. Sprinkle with cinnamon.

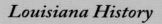

Louisiana History

New Orleans is known for its old-style coffee houses where
people eat hot beignets (see opposite page) served with rich café
au lait.

Beignets

New Orleans–style doughnuts.

Ingredients:

1 package of hot roll mix (1 pound)
¼ cup sugar
1 teaspoon vanilla
confectioners' sugar
flour
vegetable oil

Cooking utensils you'll need:
mixing bowl
measuring cups and spoons
rolling pin
large kettle for deep frying

Directions:

Prepare roll mix according to the package directions, adding the extra sugar and vanilla for added richness. When dough has risen once, punch down and cut in half. On a lightly floured surface, roll each half to make a rectangle that is 9 inches long and 12 inches wide. Cut each rectangle into 12 three-inch squares. Cover with a towel and let rise for 30 minutes. Meanwhile, fill a large cooking pot about two-thirds full of oil and heat. Oil is hot enough when dough sizzles and begins to turn brown when it is placed in the oil. (Be very careful not to burn yourself on the hot oil.) Deep fry the beignets, two at a time, for one and a half minutes on each side, until both sides are golden brown. Remove from oil and let drain on paper towels. Sprinkle generously with confectioners' sugar. Makes 2 dozen.

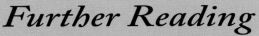

Further Reading

Ancelet, Barry Jean. *Cajun and Creole Folktales*. Jackson: University Press of Missisipi, 1994.

———— and Glen Pitre. *Cajun Country*. Jackson: University Press of Mississippi, 1991.

Folse, John D. and Craig M. Walker. *Something Old and Something New: Louisiana Cooking with a Change of Heart*. New Orleans, La.: Chef John Folse & Co, 1997.

Le Bois, Ruby. *Cajun and Creole Cookbook: The Very Best of Modern Louisiana Cooking*. New Orleans, La.: Anness, 1997.

Prudhomme, Paul. *Chef Prudhomme's Louisiana Kitchen*. New York: Morrow, 1994.

Sanna, Ellyn. *Food Folklore*. Philadelphia, Penn.: Mason Crest Publishers, 2003.

For More Information

Cajun and Creole History
www.landrystuff.com/creole.htm

Gumbo Cooking
www.gumbopages.com

Gumbo Lala
cat.xula.edu/gumbo/index.html

Louisiana Cajun and Creole
ccet.louisiana.edu

Louisiana Cooking for Kids
www.cookinglouisiana.com/
   Cooking/kids-cooking.htm

Publisher's note:
The Web sites listed on this page were active at the time of publication. The publisher is not responsible for Web sites that have changed their addresses or discontinued operation since the date of publication. The publisher will review and update the Web sites upon each reprint.

Picture Credits

Author:

Ellyn Sanna is the author of *101 Easy Supper Recipes for Busy Moms* from Promise Press, and several recipe gift books from Barbour Publishing, including *Feast, An Invitation to Tea*, and the books in the "Christmas at Home" series. A former middle school teacher and the mother of three children ages eleven through sixteen, she has experience addressing both the learning needs and the food tastes of young cooks. Ellyn Sanna has also authored and edited numerous educational titles.

Recipe Tester / Food Preparer:

Bonni Phelps caters from Vestal, New York. Her love of cooking and feeding large crowds comes from her grandmothers on both sides whom also took great pleasure in large family gatherings.

Introduction:

The Culinary Institute of America is considered the world's premier culinary college. It is a private, not-for-profit learning institution, dedicated to providing the world's best culinary education. Its campuses in New York and California provide learning environments that focus on excellence, leadership, professionalism, ethics, and respect for diversity. The institute embodies a passion for food with first-class cooking expertise.

Index

Acadia (Acadians) 8, 29, 34
Africans (African-Americans) 19, 64
American Indian 29

Beignets (New Orleans-style donuts) 66, 67
blackened food 22
Bourbon Street 59

Café au Lait 66
Cajun 21, 22, 24, 26, 28, 29, 31, 34, 35
Cajun Blackened Chicken 21
Cajun Spice Mix 24
Canada 8, 29, 34
carnival season 33, 43, 63
cayenne (history) 24
Chicken and Sausage Gumbo (recipe and history) 18, 19

Chocolate Bourbon Pecan Pie (recipe and history) 56
Chocolate Doberge Cake 53, 54, 55
crawfish legend 34
Crawfish Boulettes 35
Creole 22, 26, 27, 29, 36
Creole Vegetable and Braised Beef Stew 28

Dirty Rice 31

English (England) 8, 63
Epiphany 63

Fat Tuesday 33
French (France) 8, 29, 34, 47, 48, 55, 59, 63, 64

Germany 47
Green Salad with Creole
Vinaigrette 45

"holy trinity" 30

Jambalaya (Creole style) 36
Jesus 63

King Cake (recipe and history)
60, 61, 63

lobster legend 34

Maine 8, 34
Mardi Gras 33, 43, 44, 60, 63
metric conversion table 12

New Orleans 8, 22, 59, 64, 66,
67
New Orleans Muffaletta 40

okra 16, 18, 19, 28

Pain Perdu (French toast, recipe
and history) 48, 49
pan sizes 13
Pecan Pralines
(recipe and history) 64, 65
Plessis-Praslin, Cesar du 64
Prudhomme, Chef Paul 22

Quiche Lorraine
(recipe and history) 46, 47

Red Beans and Rice
(recipe and history) 38, 39
roux 26, 27

safety tips 10, 11
Shrimp Remoulade 32, 33
Shrimp Sauce Piquant 27
Spanish 24, 29
Strawberry Sorbet 50

Twelfth Night 33, 63